THE SIXTY MINUTE FATHER

How Time Well Spent Can Change Your Child's Life

THE SIXTY MINUTE FATHER

ROB PARSONS

BROADMAN
& HOLMAN
PUBLISHERS

Nashville, Tennessee

© 1996
by Rob Parsons

Published by
Broadman & Holman Publishers
Nashville, Tennessee
First published in Great Britain 1995
by Hodder & Stoughton, London

4262-89
0-8054-6289-9

Dewey Decimal Classification: 306.874
Subject Heading: FATHERS \ FATHER AND CHILD
Library of Congress Card Catalog Number: 96-1357

Library of Congress Cataloging-in-Publication Data

Parsons, Rob, 1948–
        The sixty minute father / Rob Parsons.
                p.   cm.
        Includes bibliographical references.
        ISBN 0-8054-6289-9
        1. Father and child. 2. Fathers–Psychology.
3. Fathers–Attitudes. 4. Parenting. I. Title.
HQ756.P385   1996
306.874'2–dc20

96-1357
CIP

00 99 98 97 96 5 4 3 2 1

12-0834G

*To our special friend, Alicia Owens—
who knew where she was going.*

Contents

Acknowledgments

Many friends have helped with *The Sixty Minute Father*. Special thanks to George Russell, Lyndon Bowring, Jonathan Booth, Jacqui Butler, Charlie Colchester, Clive Price, Helen Payton, Paul McCusker, and James Catford, my editor. My wife, Dianne, has urged me on and stopped me from taking myself too seriously. I owe her more than she knows.

Saturday Night at the Movies

We stood in line in the rain, but at last we entered the movie theater clutching two small children, a box of popcorn, and what seemed to be a gallon of cola. We were a little late and mumbled apologies as people stood to let us through to our seats. Eventually we got coats, children, Cokes, and popcorn in place. We endured ten minutes of ads and five minutes of previews until at last, the big feature. We were at the movies!

The film was *Hook,* and with a PG rating we thought, *No big scares in this one.* How wrong we were. Some fathers would later testify that the opening scene scared them more than when they were twelve and sneaked into *The Return of Dracula.*

Let me paint the picture for you. The main characters: parents, Peter and Moira; and children, Sophie and Jack.

Scene 1: The annual school play.

The hall is full of parents, most of them mothers, but in the middle of the audience is Peter, who's in his late thirties and specializes in mergers and acquisitions. He's ambitious, successful, and, one senses, a little ruthless. He's a make-it-happen kind of man.

On his right is his son, Jack, age eleven, and next to him, his wife, Moira. On stage, Sophie, age five, is putting in a credible performance as Wendy in *Peter Pan*.

It's a typical scene; video cameras are whirring, doting parents sighing, and grandmas wiping away an occasional tear. Suddenly Peter's mobile telephone rings. It's his partner Brad with news of the current deal. Peter cradles the phone to his mouth and whispers, "I can't talk–I'm at my daughter's school play." You get the sense that Brad wouldn't have been put off even if Peter had said, "I can't talk–I'm having a heart transplant." Finally Peter promises, "I'll meet you tomorrow." Just then his son turns and says, "But, Dad, it's my big baseball game–you promised to be there." Peter hesitates, then whispers into the phone, "Just a short meeting, Brad. I have to be at my boy's game." He pockets the phone and smiles at Jack, "Son, I'll be there–you have my word."

Peter doesn't mean to break his word, but the meeting with Brad goes on longer than scheduled, and he realizes he's going to be late for the game.

Cut to the ball game.

Worried mom is asking, "Where is he?" and Jack is searching the crowd with his eyes.

Enter a young junior executive: "Hello, Mrs. Brannon. Your husband is going to be a little late. He's sent me to video the parts he misses–which one's your son?"

Cut to the road outside the stadium. One hour later.

Enter Peter, tires screeching as he pulls to a stop. The stadium is empty and silent.

If his children are finding his frantic lifestyle difficult, then his wife is even more so. She is torn in at least two directions. She can see that her children are missing out on a father and that the day is coming when he'll regret these years with all his heart. When he finally arrives home, she makes a plea to him that holds a hint of despair:

"Your children love you. They want to play with you. How long do you think that will last? Soon Jack won't want you to come to his games.

"We have a few short years with our children when they actually want us around. After that, you'll be running after them for a bit of attention. It's so fast, Peter, just a few years and it's over . . . and you're missing it."

Of course, in the real world there are deadlines to meet, goals to achieve, and bills to be paid. The pressure can be colossal. Many fathers are having to put in extra-long hours just to hold on to their jobs, while others are experiencing the trauma of unemployment.

All that is true, but the sobering fact is, whatever our situation, many of us have the ability to *create unnecessary busyness*. It doesn't matter whether the demands of the job are great or small, or even if we have a job at all; we fill our lives with activity that robs us of time for things that matter.

When we live like that we are often popular outside the home. We are successful in our hobbies, honored at work, and–to our friends–the very life and soul of the party. All of that would be fine apart from the fact that so often it leads to a day when we look back on the lost opportunity of parenthood with deep regret.

The issues of over-busy lifestyles and work patterns are not limited to men; women feel these pressures just as acutely. Nevertheless, there is no doubt that in cultures all across the globe we are seeing a crisis in the role of fatherhood.

This book is designed for busy people; you can read it in about an hour. At crucial stages there are "Sixty-Second Pages" that sum up the heart of what you've just read. There is a single "One-Second Page." If you're too busy to read anything else, just read that page. If you're too busy for the "One-Second Page," you're in more trouble than you think!

Occasionally you'll find an "Action Page." I asked a number of fathers to tell me things they had done with their children that were simple yet proved to be significant in their relationship. Some are relevant to all children, others to particular age groups. Sometimes we ask, "What can I do that will begin to make a difference?" You may find some ideas on the "Action Pages."

The lessons I share are born not of success but of failure, although I am thankful that I learned some of them before it was too late for my own family. I remember coming home from work and sitting at the dinner table. My wife had long since given up trying to communicate with me at that hour of the day, but my two small children hadn't.

"Dad, I'm on the football team on Saturday."

"Susan pulled my hair again today!"

But I was distant, my mind still with a client or planning the evening's strategy. I would mumble a reply. Then the telephone would ring and a small boy would say, "Dad, it's for you." Suddenly I would come alive, animated as I talked. And my two young children would watch me. They weren't stamping or kicking; it would have been better for me if they had been. But the message they were getting loud and clear was, *This matters to him. This brings him alive.*

Changing that kind of lifestyle is, for me, an on-going battle; this book contains some of the lessons I am learning along the way.

I know there will be some fathers reading this book who would love to give their children more time but are separated from them because of family break-up. I do not presume that all of this book will be relevant to your situation, but I hope parts of it will apply and will help to make whatever time you have with your child as fruitful as possible.

The role of fatherhood is not an easy one, and there are no guarantees as to how our children will turn out. Having said that, I feel there will come a time when each of us will look back and want to know that we have given this task our very best effort.

In this book there are ten goals that will help you and me in that aim. Each of them is a powerful tool in the work of a father, and each has the potential to change your life and the lives of your children–forever.

Goal 1
"Seize the Day"

A Window of Opportunity

Vincent Foster was a lawyer—but not just any lawyer. He had risen to the peak of his profession as deputy counsel to the president of the United States. He was one of the most powerful lawyers in the world. During his term of office he addressed the graduating class of University of Arkansas School of Law.

Imagine the crowded lecture hall; picture the several hundred students anxious to hear from the man they so wanted to emulate. Let's slip in at the back of that class and listen to some of what he said that day.

Three weeks ago my wife, Lisa, and I celebrated our twenty-fifth wedding anniversary, and it was here in Fayetteville at the University of Arkansas Law School where we celebrated our first. Like many in this audience, she began by putting me through law school, and for twenty-two years she always encouraged me to persevere and to aim higher. She has been my editor, my jury consultant, and my best friend. I wish for each of you a Lisa.

The lecture hall was still, as if the words being spoken were somehow above the mere consideration of the law. He went on.

A word about family. You have amply demonstrated that you are achievers willing to work hard, long hours and set aside your personal lives. But it reminds me of that observation that no one was ever heard to say on their deathbed, "I wish I had spent more time at the office." Balance wisely your professional life and your family life. If you are fortunate to have children, your parents will warn you that they will grow up and be gone before you know it. I can testify that it is true. God only allows us so many opportunities with our children to read a story, go fishing, play catch, and say our prayers together. Try not to miss one of them. The office can wait. It will still be there after your children are gone.

Six weeks later, Vince Foster was dead. His life had ended in tragic circumstances. Official verdict: suicide.

Who knows what traumas beset that man in the final months of his life. But as I read the words he had spoken that day, they seemed to come to me from another world. I understand so clearly what he said to those young lawyers but not just because I, too, am a lawyer. I remember the day when it dawned on me that, although by most standards I was successful, those I really loved were slipping through my hands.

My background was not dissimilar to that of Vince Foster. My parents were not well-off, and my wife, too, had worked to help me through law school. I had become a joint senior partner in a successful law firm, a speaker on management issues, in demand both at home and abroad, yet my children were growing up without me. I told myself that I was doing it all for them, but they would have preferred fewer luxuries and more of me. One day it came home to me that unless I changed, both I myself and my family were going to pay a price that I would regret for the rest of my life.

Action Page

⇨ Put dates in your diary that are important to your children: birthdays, school concerts, sports events.

⇨ Get involved with your newborn baby as much as possible. Change as many diapers as you can, and hold her in your arms often. Talk to her as if she can understand every word.

⇨ Start a hobby or leisure activity with your child that is not dependent on physical fitness. You may do it together for the rest of your life.

A Father Looks Back

A father sat and flipped through a family album. His children were almost adults, and the day when the home was free of untidy bedrooms and blaring music was closer than he wanted. It was not an outstanding collection of great photographic skill, and occasionally whole heads had been cut off in a photo. Nevertheless, this was a record of the years.

Not an organized album, this one: nobody had in the suggested manner written the date and place on the back of each photograph. Eighteen years of home life were randomly thrown together. Yet one still could read in those memories the unmistakable journey this family had made together through the years.

There was a toddler with a broad smile that showed no hint of embarrassment that he had just one tooth. Two children played on a beach. A shepherd clung grimly to a stuffed lamb in a nativity play that even a kind critic would have described as low-budget. A woman sat on a wall flanked by three children—one smiling beautifully, another squinting in the sun, and a third making a face. There were Christmases, aunts and uncles, birthdays, and enough animals for a small zoo.

Then the father sighed and reached for a photograph tucked into the sleeve of the album. Smiling out of the photograph was a young man. He stood in what obviously was a hospital room, and in his hands he cradled a newborn baby. He had built up a business, sat on numerous boards and committees, and had, without a doubt, achieved what some would call success. As he gazed at the photograph, his shoulders sagged. Finally he lifted his head and whispered, "I would trade it all today if I could roll back the years and begin again."

I have met that father so many times in a thousand different locations. Wherever I have lectured in the world, he has been there. He may be a business executive, plumber, university lecturer, or factory worker. Is he a bad father? Is it that he doesn't care about his children? No, in many ways he is a good father. He loves his family. He provides for them and tries to give them the very best. If you asked him which was more important—his work, his hobbies, or his family—he would answer in a moment, "My wife, my children." Yet he is fifty years old, his family is grown, and he feels he has missed their very childhood.

This man understands the phrase "windows of opportunity." He hates to miss a single one of them. It means a chance to do something; it could be the opportunity to net an important customer, develop some new technology, or open up sales opportunities in a new market.

The incredible thing is that so many fathers who have never missed a window of opportunity in their jobs or careers pass by the window of childhood as if it will never close.

Count the Days

How wide is that window? The truth is, if we don't spend time with our children when they are small, they probably won't spend time with us when they are teen-agers. But let's be easy on ourselves and assume we have until they are eighteen to build a strong relationship with them. Those eighteen years of our children's lives contain 6,570 days. Each day may hold the opportunity to spend time with them, to pass on values that matter to us, or to just teach them how to fly a kite.

I occasionally have had to visit clients in prison. Such visits are normally in an interview room, but I remember on one occasion seeing some numbers scratched into the wall of a cell. A man had lived in this cell for ten long years, and as he went to bed each night, he scratched a line. Every one of them represented a day—twenty-four hours less to serve.

It is impossible for us to live our lives with such a compelling sense of the passage of time. But with the pressures of modern life it's easy to have the opposite problem; we just don't realize how fast those days are passing.

There's hardly a father on the face of the earth who would contemplate missing the opportunity to build strong relationships with his children—if he realized what was happening. But so often we don't, and the years slip by a day at a time.

Carpe Diem—Seize the Day!

Remember those old school photographs several decades ago? Once a year the man with the camera came and tried to get four hundred children in one shot. He did it by using a camera that revolved. It would begin at one end of the line and move its way along a sea of young faces.

A classmate, Rowland Thompson, discovered that such an instrument gave schoolboys a wonderful possibility. I was in the restroom as he described his plan, and I was privileged to be one of the four hundred as he executed it. The second the camera had panned Rowland's glowing visage, he ran around the back of the group to the other end of the line . . . and got his face in the photo twice.

I was also there when Rowland emerged from the principal's office, head held high. Neither lashing with tongue nor cane had quelled that indomitable spirit as he whispered, "It was worth it."

We all have gazed at our old school photographs. Pupils of years gone by look out at us—heroes, bullies, clowns—all smiling as if that moment would last forever; as if time would never ask them to swap school uniform for suit or coveralls, never demand that chewing gum be exchanged for in-baskets, never require them to hand in the water pistol and collect a business plan.

The Promise of Tomorrow

There is a similar scene in the film *Dead Poets Society*. A group of teenage children and their teacher walk along a school corridor lined with old photographs. Dozens of young people, captured on film, stare out of the frames; faces full of potential, lives at the very start of a journey. But many are now dead, ravaged by wars in Germany, France, and Vietnam.

The normally boisterous pupils are silent as they gaze back into time at the faces of previous generations, and their teacher whispers in their ears the Latin phrase *Carpe Diem*. It means "seize the day"—simply that none of our tomorrows are guaranteed and we need to make the most of every opportunity *today*.

> *Gather ye rosebuds while ye may,*
> *Old time is still a flying,*
> *And that same flower that smiles today,*
> *Tomorrow will be dying.*[1]
>
> —Robert Herrick

The "Carpe Diem" principle is nowhere more true than in fatherhood. This is because the door of childhood closes so quickly and so finally. One of the reasons we don't spend quality time with our children is that, when they are small, we believe there will always be tomorrow. That single mistake allows us to go through their childhood years saying, "Later," "Tomorrow," "Next week," or "I'm sorry, I know I promised. but I'll play next time."

During those years, the door of childhood is wide open. They want to spend time with us; often they don't even want us to *do* things with them, they just want us *to be there*. During those times, their minds are open. In those early years, we have the opportunity to pass on to them the things that matter to us. It's a time to tell them what we believe.

It's when we are young that we learn the lessons that form the basis for a whole life.

In his book *All I Really Need to Know I Learned in Kindergarten,*[2] Robert Fulghum highlights how the lessons learned in those early years can create a foundation for the whole of life.

> *All I really need to know about how to live and what to do and how to be I learned in kindergarten. Wisdom was not at the top of the graduate-school mountain, but there in the sandpile at Sunday School.*

The Lessons of the Sandpile

Share everything.

Play fair.

Don't hit people.

Put things back where you found them.

Clean up your own mess.

Don't take things that aren't yours.

Say you're sorry when you hurt somebody.

Wash your hands before you eat.

Flush.

Warm cookies and cold milk are good for you.

Live a balanced life—learn some, and think some, and draw and paint and sing and dance and play and work every day some.

Take a nap every afternoon.

When you go out into the world, watch out for traffic, hold hands, and stick together.

Be aware of wonder. Remember the little seed in the styrofoam cup: the roots go down and the plant goes up and nobody really knows how or why, but we are all like that.

Goldfish and hamsters and white mice and even the little seed in the styrofoam cup—they all die. So do we.

And then remember the Dick and Jane books and the first word you learned—the biggest word of all: LOOK.

Action Page

⇨ Children love receiving letters. If you have to be away from home, drop them a line.

⇨ Read aloud to your children.

⇨ Tell your children every day that you love them. Show physical affection as often as possible.

The Closing Door of Childhood

If you have young children, let me mention something about the teenage years that may be waiting to ambush you. Now, your children pour out their hearts to you–then, they may grunt. Now, they love to hold your hand in the street–then, they may not want to be seen dead with you. Now, they go to bed at nine–then, you may wait up half the night wondering if you'll ever see them again. You may think their bedroom is untidy now, but then, you may need a tetanus shot before you go in.

But if all this is true, it is also true that if you listen to them when they are five, six, or seven, there's a chance they'll listen to you when they are fifteen, sixteen, or seventeen.

My son, Lloyd, used to come into the bathroom in the mornings and say, "Dad, tell me a story while you're shaving." We had an imaginary character named Tommy who would have great escapades. Lloyd's favorite was when the school bully picked on Tommy, not knowing that, in fact, he was a long-lost twin . . . who just happened to be a karate expert.

Lloyd asked for those stories every day. Then one day he didn't come. He didn't send me a postcard to warn me this was going to happen. He didn't even say, "By the way, Dad, this morning is the last one." One rainy winter's day at 7:00 A.M. that particular door silently closed.

That was one opportunity to tell a story and spend a little time together, but the principle holds true for all those childhood experiences. These are times when our children want to be with us, to hear what we think, to ask questions that matter to them and hear answers that matter to us.

Nobody sums up how fast those opportunities pass as well as Harry Chapin in "Cat's in the Cradle."[3] It's a song about a boy who every day asked his father to spend time with him:

> *"When you comin' home, Dad?"*
> *"I don't know when*
> *but we'll get together then—*
> *you know, we'll have a good time then."*

But his father is a busy man: "There are planes to catch and bills to pay." As the song goes on, the child moves from a toddler to a ten-year-old, saying, "Thanks for the ball, Dad, come on let's play." His father promises that very soon they'll have time together.

And then it happens; time plays its trick and suddenly the boy is a man. Now the father has time— but the door is closed.

> *Well, he came home from college just the other day,*
> *so much like a man I just had to say,*
> *"Son, I'm proud of you, can you sit for a while?"*
> *He shook his head and said with a smile—*
> *"What I'd really like, Dad, is to borrow the car keys,*
> *see you later, can I have them please?"*
> . . . .
> *"When you comin' home, Son?"*
> *"I don't know when,*

but we'll get together then, Dad,
you know, we'll have a good time then."

There are few of us who won't feel guilty when we consider these issues. There is no doubt that the time we spend with our children in their early years is vital, but the good news is, whatever age—whether they are three or thirty-three—we can make a difference in their lives. Many a man has discovered a relationship with his father years after leaving home. But even at that stage of life the same two ingredients are needed as when our children were small: time and the courage to seize the day.

Let's consider those eighteen years of childhood again and imagine for a moment that an hourglass contains not sand but days. When your child was born, the timer had in it 6,570 days. If your child is ten years old, 3,650 days have already gone. You have 2,920 left. No amount of money, power, or prestige can increase that number.

Vince Foster was right—"Don't miss one of them."

The Sixty-Second Page

⏰ No one was ever heard to say on their deathbed, "I wish I had spent more time at the office."

⏰ The door of childhood closes so quickly and so finally.

⏰ In those early years we have the opportunity to pass on to our children the things that matter to us. It's a time to tell them what we believe.

⏰ If we listen to them when they are five, six, or seven, they may listen to us when they're fifteen, sixteen, or seventeen.

⏰ If your child is ten years old, 3,650 days have already gone. You have 2,920 left.

⏰ Vince Foster was right—"Try not to miss one of them."

Take a Breather

There is hardly a father who wouldn't say, "I agree! I want to spend as much time with my family as possible." The problem is, of course, we just don't have enough time. Let's face it—with your busy schedule, even reading this far has taken commitment. So how can the space be created to give even more time to the task of building strong relationships with your children?

It would be wonderful if we could walk into our boss's office or write to the shareholders and say, "Good news! I'm going to be a better parent. That means I'll be working less hours, and, by the way, don't call me at home." The problem is, the real world doesn't stop for us to catch up on the task of being an effective father. The truth is, there are many demands on our time that we can't do much about, but so often the biggest time pressure is the unnecessary busyness that *we* create.

The next goal will help us deal with this because it urges us to deal with three great illusions. Each of them is powerful, but the last is utterly devastating in its ability to rob us of time for the things that matter. In that sense it is in a class of its own; I have called it "The Greatest Illusion of All."

When I was a boy of fourteen, my father was so ignorant I could hardly stand to have him around. But when I got to be twenty-one, I was astonished at how much the old man had learned.

–Mark Twain

Goal 2
To Dispel
the Illusions

Illusion 1 – "I have no choice"

It's 10:50 A.M. You are in the fast lane on the highway and have just thirty minutes to get to your meeting. The road seems reasonably clear, and the fog that had dogged you has evaporated. And then you see it. You glance at your fuel gauge and see it's nudging empty. You get a sick feeling in the pit of your stomach, but as you lift your eyes back to the road, you see a sign announcing that there's a service station a mile ahead. You drop your speed, move into the slow lane, then suddenly change your mind. You mutter to yourself, "I've got enough to get me there. I'll fill up after the meeting." You sail past the service station.

And you almost make it. If it hadn't been for that traffic jam you would have gotten there. As it is, you are trudging along the highway, gas can in hand, with all hope of making the meeting long since gone. You ask yourself, "Why didn't I stop back there?" The answer to that question may lie a little deeper than the time pressure; it could be found in your *personality.*

Some of us have a personality type that leads us into a certain lifestyle. See if you relate to any of the following characteristics that identify those of us who live this way.

We do things quickly. We walk fast, talk fast, and drive fast—even on vacation. It's a sunny afternoon; the whole world seems to be enjoying rowing slowly down the lazy river. Except for us. We have decided to race the ducks, the woman walking on the bank, and the man in a boat further up the river. We alone are making waves!

We are very competitive. We compete over everything and find to our embarrassment that even when playing board games with small children we are desperately trying to win.

We cannot resist a telephone ringing. The worst thing in life that can happen to us is to get to the telephone just as it stops ringing. If that happens, we begin to call people, asking, "Was that you trying to get me a moment ago?"

We swap lanes in traffic jams—even though we know that there is an eternal law that the lane we have just joined will now move more slowly than the lane we have just left.

When driving down highways we are constantly working out complicated mathematical sums—"Atlanta is ninety miles away. If I drive at 90 mph it will take me an hour. If I drive at 180 mph it will take me half an hour. If I drive at 70 mph . . . no, that's too difficult."

We are fascinated by numbers. The first thing we do when we get in a car at the beginning of a long journey is set the trip odometer. We don't do anything with that number; we just like to know *how far we've been.*

We polyphase. That means we do lots of things at once. We may be reading our child a bedtime story while on the phone to a customer and at the same time completing our expense form.

We find it hard to relax and often get sick on vacation.

And would you believe it . . .

We hate stopping for gas. Why do we hate it so much? It's because when we pull in at the service station, we watch as all the cars and trucks we had overtaken pass us.

Of course, very few people have all those characteristics, but most of us have some. Actually that kind of lifestyle is not conducive to effectiveness either at work or at home. But there's something even more interesting. Such people tend to have another characteristic . . .

. . . they work long hours—
regardless of the need.

Knowing Ourselves

Everybody has to work long hours sometimes. We can't always put family first. There are overtime hours to work, reports to write, accounts to call on.

Occasions when we can't spend as much time with our children as we'd like are bearable if we know there's no other way. The real tragedy is when the pressure is self-imposed and we are literally robbed of quality time with our families by false "busyness" that we create ourselves. This happens when we work late on Friday so we can have the weekend off. But we don't quite finish, and we go in on Saturday morning "just for a few hours." We find that we're still there at five and decide to bring some work home for Sunday so we can have a clear desk on Monday.

All of that would be fine except for the fact that we've lived like this for fifteen years; long hours have become a way of life and we work them regardless of the needs of the job. In truth they are fulfilling a need in *us*.

One of the signs of a motivated employee is that he or she is prepared to put in extra hours when the chips are down. But the big question is whether we work long hours *regardless of need*. Why are long hours so attractive? It's because they say to us, *What a great job you're doing—how would we ever get by without you?*

I spoke recently to somebody who said, "In our office we dare not go home at six even if all the work is done. There's an unwritten rule that you hang around until eight and go home looking weary."

Can this be true? Is it possible that we could be getting up from our desk at five—it looks as if we'll get to that school concert after all—then stop and say to ourselves, "I'll just slip down the corridor to see if that fax has arrived. Perhaps I'll just make one more phone call"?

In themselves, long hours don't prove a thing; they are certainly no indication of what we achieve. James Ling summed it up when he said, "Don't tell me how long you work, tell me what you get done."

Last-Choice Children

Jim was made redundant at his office at age forty-three. The job he found two years later required him to work a sixty-hour week. He didn't choose that. There are plenty of events that happen in our working lives that cause us to work extra hours, get home exhausted, and go straight back out again. None of us can do much about those times in our lives. The problem comes when we *choose* to live that way.

One of the first things we say when we come through the door is, "Any calls for me?" We like to be active, and although we might not admit it, we create busyness. And there's the key to it. Some of us need the busyness. It's not just our jobs that keep us from our children—we say "yes" to almost anybody who asks us to do anything. We love to be busy; we want to be wanted.

So often those of us who say "yes" to the whole world end up saying "no" to those who are closest to us and who need us more than anybody else.

Janice was a seventeen-year-old girl whose father had died when she was eight. She noticed when she went to the houses of friends that although some had close relationships with their fathers, many seemed to be in the same situation as she. Then she realized that these children had not lost their fathers to death but to a self-imposed busyness. This is part of what she wrote:

> *Mom has coped amazingly well and I'm so very proud of her. Occasionally, though, it does make me sad to think what I'm missing out on, especially when I hear other fathers talk about those special moments. However, I know that if Daddy were alive, he would be an amazing father. What really upsets me are those fathers who have* chosen not to be with their children.

Can Janice be right? She was robbed of her father's time by death, but is it possible for children to have their father's presence in a home yet not have *him?* Is it possible that good fathers who love their children *choose not to be with them?*

Yes, it is possible, because to rich and poor, clever and dull, a limited amount of time is given, and every choice we make precludes another. An Eastern proverb sums it up like this: "If you do this you can't do that." Such choices are often not major issues, but they are made one at a time and built into a lifestyle. They could even be as simple as a telephone call.

A Modern Parable

The young couple walked out of the hospital together. He was carrying a small bundle that weighed just six pounds and around which a battle was still raging over selection of a name. He was prouder than he had ever been in his whole life.

His wife stepped into the car first, and he reached in to pass the baby to her. And then it happened. The car phone rang. To this day he can't remember why he did it, but he took one hand from the child and reached for the handset. For a moment, as if frozen in time, the child was suspended, balancing on the palm of one hand. His wife screamed; he took his hand from the phone and clutched the baby. Whoever was calling hung up.

The telephone lost the battle that day, but it vowed at that very moment that never again would this new child take priority. It planned a campaign that would rob this father of time with his child.

That was eighteen years ago, and since that moment the phone has always rung just when a bedtime story was getting exciting or when a game of Monopoly was drawing to a close or, in later years, when a father and his teenager were at the start of some crucial conversation. The phone had always promised the man that it would not take much of his time and that he could soon return to whatever he was doing. In all those years, the father had never spotted the strategy. The phone had never lost once.

When the child left home at eighteen, the phone stopped ringing. The revenge was complete.

That parable strikes a chord in my experience. When my daughter was very young she would love me to read to her before she went to sleep. It always seemed that, just as we were getting to the most exciting part of the story, the phone would ring. She would say, "Oh, Dad, let it ring." She may as well have asked me to fly. "I'll only be a moment," I'd say as I rushed out of her room and descended the stairs two at a time.

The one call often led to another, but eventually I would remember I hadn't gotten the frog back into a prince and I would rush upstairs. But little eyes had fought to stay awake as long as they could. I had chosen.

I could have chosen otherwise. In my life I've had thousands of business calls. Many of them have been described to me as "urgent," but I can count on one hand those that really couldn't wait twenty minutes.

We are used to looking at demands and deciding their level of priority depending on who asks us to do them. We are inclined to give attention first to the demands of our boss, close friend, or most important customer. Their phone calls tend to get returned promptly and, whatever the pressure, we make time for them.

The problem for children is that they do not have the power of bosses, customers, or colleagues. Whether it's a bedtime story with a toddler, making a model airplane with a ten-year-old, or helping a teenager with a history project, we can easily put them off with, "We'll do it tomorrow."

The Forty Second Father

In one survey of fathers,[4] the men were asked, "How long do you think you spend each day in conversation with your toddlers?" Most guessed between fifteen and twenty minutes a day. To test this, the researchers put microphones on the fathers and their children to measure accurately the amount of parental interaction. Those busy men spent on average less than forty seconds a day with their children, split into three encounters of between ten and fifteen seconds each. In another survey,[5] fathers were spending three minutes a day talking with their children, but the research also showed that the children were watching three *hours* of television a day.

Action Page

➩ Kneel to talk to toddlers and listen with your *eyes*.

➩ As children get older, respect their privacy.
Knock on their bedroom door before entering,
and never search their rooms or read their
diaries unless it's vital.

➩ Go with your teenager to listen to his or her
favorite band. Listen to some of the group's
music the week before—it will help you through
the pain barrier!

The Wealthy Pauper

I remember once speaking to five young men. I'd spent three hours advising them on a strategy to help build their business. When I finished, I said, "Do you mind if I ask you something?" (Frankly, I was going to ask it whether they minded or not.) "Are any of you married with children?" They all were. I said, "My great fear for you is that in ten years you'll be even wealthier than you are now, but you will have lived those years as paupers."

One of them said, "I know what you mean." He went on, "My alarm goes off at five thirty; I like to be in the office at seven. The other day, by mistake, it went off at eight, and I was stamping around the house angrily. My six-year-old boy said, 'What are you doing home at this time of day, Dad? Will you take me to school?' I held his hand and we kicked leaves together on the way to his school." He said, "I thought to myself, *Why don't I do this more often?*"

It may be because he can't, and it could be that, even without knowing it, he chooses.

Illusion 2 – "I'm busy all day"

"You have no idea how busy I am," the man yelled. "I would love to have time for all this, but I just don't– I'm busy all day."

Isn't that a fascinating phrase–"busy all day"? But what does it mean? In an average life we spend six months waiting for traffic lights to change, twenty-three years asleep, and two years looking for things. Of course, the big worry is that by the time we've had a nap, looked for our favorite tie, and waited for a green light, there won't be time to do much else.

Without a doubt, time is both a precious and a diminishing asset. It is an unusual commodity. We can't rent it, buy it, mortgage it; we can't even save it, because as soon as we do, it's gone. We can only spend it. Some of the shrewdest business people in the world have discovered that it's a hard asset to control.

A Tale of a Man Called Joe

Joe Sunderland is a factory foreman. The job involves a lot of paperwork, as well as direct contact with the workforce. Like everybody in the world who has an office, Joe has in the corner of his a "problem file." It's been there for about nine months and has grown in gruesomeness over that period. He believes that if he goes to it now, gremlins will leap out and devour him. Actually, if he tackled it with some real effort, in three hours he'd have it sorted.

Almost every Monday morning for the past six months, Joe has determined to tackle that file, but life has been so busy, he hasn't had time; it was just too easy to do something else. That was until Wednesday, when he received a letter from the main office saying that if they didn't get an answer in seven days he should be sure not to give up his evening job! The following day, Joe gets in at 7:00 A.M. to tackle the file.

He has four hours in which to do it before his first meeting at 11.00 A.M. Let's watch what happens.

Scene 1. The office.

7:00 A.M. Joe sits at his desk, glances at the file, and mutters, "I'll just have a quick cup of coffee to get me going." He wanders down the corridor to the drink machine. Susan is there. They begin to chat . . .

7:40 A.M. He's back at his desk when his eye spots a phone message: "Call Mr. Tompkins." That message has been there for two days. He thinks, *If I can get him off my back I can really concentrate on that file.*

8:50 A.M. Tompkins was long and irate. Joe decides to call his boss to discuss it. But first he needs the papers. His secretary isn't in yet, so he begins to rifle the filing cabinets . . .

9:20 A.M. He calls the main office.

9:50 A.M. Bill pops his head in the door and asks, "Can you spare me a minute?" (If anyone ever says that to you, they're lying.) Joe smiles, "Sure come on in—I was about to have a break anyway."

10:25 A.M. Bill leaves. Jim thinks, *No point in starting it now,* and turns to a pile of phone messages.

4:00 P.M. "I'll call the main office and explain that I haven't been able to start it yet. I've been busy all day."

4:05 P.M. Main office is less than sympathetic.

Scene 2. The hall of Joe's home.

Joe comes through the door. His son has been waiting for an hour.

7:15 P.M. "Where have you been, Dad? The game starts in fifteen minutes!"

"I'm really sorry, Son. Something big has come up, a major hassle at the factory. I have to go back in, work on a problem file, and get a fax off to the main office tonight."

"Joe, you promised him–he's been waiting for you since he came home from school."

"Listen–none of you understand the pressure I'm under. I've been busy all day."

An Account of a Man Called George

By the time Joe started work on that Thursday, another man, on the other side of the country, was already well into his morning; but even by then, George Bush had no idea what the rest of the day held in store.

By 11 A.M. the USSR had broken up; the CIA wanted to put a thousand agents in before it changed again. Saddam Hussein had deported a third team of observers, and Israel had said, "No loans–no peace conference." Everybody wanted him to air an opinion on it or send troops to get rid of it.

He cannot remember a busier seven hours. But at 4:00 in the afternoon George was playing golf. At dinner Barbara asked him, "What kind of a day have you had, dear?"

"Awful!" said George, "I dropped a shot on the ninth."

Did Joe or George have the busiest day? Who can tell? But I know this: only one man did what he intended to do that day—at work and at play. And he did it with a combination of three things—effective use of time, planning, and sheer will power.

The price that Joe's family paid that night was not necessary. He could have done the work and made the big match. In truth he created the busyness that robbed him of those hours. And the double tragedy is that those evenings are limited. George Bush isn't president now, but people still want to play golf with him.

Let's hope Joe's as lucky with his ten-year-old.

Illusion 3—"The Greatest Illusion of All"

The managing director of the marketing company made his way to the flip chart and began the presentation to his six key employees; these were the brightest, the most innovative, the elite of the advertising world.

Among this group was the woman who had coined the slogan that tripled the sales of a soft-drink company, and lounging in the second row was the man who had come up with the phrase that pushed a secondary bank into the top ten lenders.

He paused for silence and began. "Our client on this job is anonymous, and the task itself is unusual.

We are asked to conceive a plan that will encourage fathers to spend *less* time with their children."

"Easy!" yelled a voice from the back. "Give them a job here."

The managing director frowned and went on, "You must work as individuals. You have one week to formulate your plan. The prize—a seat on the board. We meet next Wednesday, 10:00 A.M. sharp."

A week later, at 2:00 A.M. on the very morning of the meeting, it happened. Charles had spent seven long days, smoked three hundred cigarettes, used ten legal pads, and had all but given up. Then in a moment it had come to him—a phrase so simple, so appealing, so devastating in its effectiveness that he knew he had won. He smiled as he switched off the light and determined to make his presentation last.

Seven hours later he was waiting for the meeting to start and gazing around the board room at the competition. He smiled as he noticed that most of his colleagues were huddling an art board closely to their chests, as if at the last moment a rival would copy their brilliance. Finally, the managing director announced that the presentations were to begin. Jim went first. "We'll tell the fathers that the long hours are for the sake of the kids. Good holidays, computer games, designer clothes." And then he unveiled it . . . "Dad's away because he wants the best for you."

The managing director wasn't impressed and coughed in embarrassment. These, after all, were his best people. The next showed more promise. "The heart of my campaign is to elevate work above the family. 'Modern man—working to improve all our tomorrows.'"

There was a retching sound from the second row as somebody pretended to be sick. Eventually five of the team had shared their very best ideas. The prospects of telling the client they needed more time and sacking half his workforce were dueling for space in the managing director's mind when number six took the podium.

Charles stood and smiled, and before he opened his mouth, they knew he had done it. They had seen that smile on one other occasion. It was just before he unveiled the idea that put an ailing politician back in office despite every poll in the country being against him.

He said, "We'll tell fathers that their families need them, that the time with their children is short and the door of childhood closes so quickly and so finally. And we'll tell them if they don't give time now, then years later they'll regret it with all their hearts."

The managing director shuffled and wondered whether the major insanity was in him or the team, but number six went on . . .

"And we'll tell them to make sure they carve out quality time with their families." He paused for effect.

"But we'll say that life is busy right now, so make plans for tomorrow." And then with a flourish he unveiled it. The managing director beamed; the rest of the team gasped in disappointment . . .

. . . "A slower day is coming."

It was the promise of the slower day that allowed the father in "Cat's in the Cradle" to say, "We'll have a good time . . . then." It's the hope that when the business is established, when the new computer is up and running, when the rush job is finished, when the house is decorated . . . then we'll have time.

It will revolutionize our lives if we realize that the slower day is not coming. It's "The Greatest Illusion" because so often we create busyness *from within*.

If we are going to make a difference as fathers, we need to do it *now*. That decision is practical. It has to do with bedtimes, Saturday football games, stories, and hamburgers; and it has to do with carving those times out of busy lives–today.

Ray was a good lecturer; he gave himself to the college. There were papers to mark, meetings to chair, and problems to sort out, but he always believed that next week would be easier. He had believed it for thirty years. One day the slower day came. The dean and all his colleagues thanked him for every one of those thirty years. Ironic that they gave him a clock.

The Sixty-Second Page

⏰ "Don't tell me how long you work—tell me what you get done."

⏰ "What really upsets me are those fathers *who have chosen* not to be with their children."
>   —Janice, 17, who lost her father
>   when she was 8

⏰ "The problem for children is that they don't have the power of bosses, customers, or colleagues."

⏰ "Only one man did what he intended to do that day—by effective use of time, planning, and sheer will power."

The One-Second Page

Remember "The Greatest Illusion of All" and believe . . .

The slower day is not coming!

Being a Good Father— the Very Last Word

When it comes to being a good father, only one word matters. If you and I succeed in this, it won't matter much that we haven't been textbook fathers or that we feel we've blown it in a hundred other ways. In spite of all that we've said about the importance of giving them time, you could be a father who has to be away a great deal, but if you capture the heart of this word you will not only enjoy your children but give them a security which will last a lifetime.

And when your child is an adult, looks back on her younger years, and considers whether or not you were a good father, she will judge you by this simple word. The next eight goals are dedicated to it . . .

. . . Relationship.

Action Page

⇨ Designate an evening as "television free" and plan to do something creative together.

⇨ Whenever possible try not to take phone calls during times you have set aside for your children.

⇨ Develop family traditions. These could be as simple as cooking hamburgers every Saturday night–your children look forward to them and remember them when they are grown.

Goal 3
To Give Love
without Strings

Come back in time with me for a moment. You are dressed in short trousers, have an unforgettable haircut, and look just as you do in the photograph your mother has on top of the sideboard. You are ten years old.

You are standing in a school playground. Try to imagine the scene. Two boys are leaning against a wall gazing out at a large group of children. Their eyes are searching, assessing; they are picking teams.

"I'll have Peter."

"I'll take Graham."

Your stomach is churning as the awful possibility dawns that you could be chosen last. The names continue to be called: "Harry!" "Mark!" "Jim!" "Michael!" You are beginning to feel sick.

Then finally—your name! You saunter across the great divide that separates the wanted from the rest, and you realize just one boy—with eyes lowered—now stands behind you. And you know you need never have worried because he is always picked last.

How did the two captains choose? Friendship may have counted for something; maybe even a little bribery—a trading card or two—may have affected the decision. But, without a doubt, the main factor was ability. They wanted winners on their team.

Most of us have never left that playground. The two captains are long since gone, only to be replaced by foremen, bosses, colleagues, and shareholders. And we know that if we achieve they'll want us.

Since the playground, we have been taught that if we succeed, people will like us, even love us. Pretty babies get the most attention, grandmas are wheeled out to listen to the most gifted child play her violin; we are given rewards when we succeed. But a father's love should be different.

A Life Principle

The key to a child's heart is to let her know that she is loved no matter what. There is no more powerful force on the face of the earth for building strong relationships than unconditional love.

I learned that lesson the hard way. I remember my daughter coming home from school. She came running in yelling, "Dad, I got a ninety-five on my math test." I had two questions for my little girl: "What happened to the other five points?" and "Where were you in the class order?"

I'm not proud of that memory. Katie has a whole life in front of her filled with those who will want her when she succeeds. I want to motivate her to be the best she can be. But more than that, I want her to know that my love for her is based not on success but on the fact that I am her father.

A friend opened my eyes to it all. I heard how he had dealt with his son who had done well in his exams. The conversation went like this:

> *"Well, Son, don't keep us all in suspense—what does the letter say?"*
>
> *"I passed them all, Dad—six of them with A's."*
>
> *"I am so proud of you. You have worked incredibly hard—you deserve it. But I also want to take this moment to remind you of what I think you know already. I don't love you any* more *because you did well. I love you anyway. If you had come home having failed them all, I would have been disappointed but I wouldn't have loved you less. You must never forget that.* It is a life principle between you and me."

Unconditional Love

I remember a man coming to me at the end of a seminar. I listened carefully as he poured out his story to me, although I had heard the heart of it many times before, from so many men. He recounted the time he had run home from school and told his father that he had finished second in the whole county on his music exam. He said, "My father asked, 'Won't you ever come in first?'"

He said, "I am nearly fifty years of age. I am responsible for two hundred staff, I have children of my own, and I am still trying to prove myself to my father."

When we love unconditionally, we communicate acceptance. We may have won fifty tennis matches, but we don't bring our son down because he couldn't return a tennis ball to save his life. Our daughter may weigh more than we would like, and she has to take plenty of ridicule at her school, but she is never the butt of *our* jokes.

The children of such a father know that, whether they win the race or come in last, whether they are fat or thin, achieve distinctions or fail, they are loved. Our commitment to them is not based on their success but on our *relationship*.

A friend of mine was recently at a very unusual school awards ceremony. It was not the principal that made it unusual; he stood up and, in time-honored fashion, read out the list of those who had achieved in outstanding ways. It was not the prizes that set this occasion apart; the usual display of books and certificates was in evidence. And it was not even the children, although it has to be said that this was not a typical school assembly.

No, it was the *achievements* that made this particular awards ceremony so different. As the principal read them out, no one present had any doubt that the feats these teenage children had performed were outstanding. Yet everybody knew there was hardly a child of any age, in any school in the country, that could not have done any one of them.

The audience listened as the principal read the names and reasons why these particular pupils had won a prize. "Mark, because he fed himself all term; and Richard, because he has learned to blow his nose; and Susan, who has recited a poem and can brush her teeth."

The school was one which cared for severely disabled children. As some shuffled and others danced to collect their trophies, there was hardly a dry eye in the place. Yet this was more than just emotion; it was somehow a spiritual event, almost of another world. Why was it so different?

I think the answer is clear. In our society we are used to award ceremonies. They are occasions when we acknowledge those who have out-performed the normal man, woman, or child. We may spend our lives in a drama group, but most of us will never skip up the steps of a stage in Los Angeles to collect an Oscar. There are thousands of us who at some time in our lives have run for all we were worth at a school sports day, but few of us will stand on a winner's platform clutching a gold medal as the world sings our national anthem.

No, most award ceremonies are for the few that the rest of us would love to be like. The ceremony at this school was for those with whom most of us would never want to change places, yet they were accepted and honored.

At the back of the auditorium, fathers cheered and clapped and yelled encouragements. Would those fathers have preferred to have been watching their sons and daughters as winners breaking the tape at a local school's sports day? Probably. But they have learned that the heart of a father's love is *acceptance*.

Come with me to another place. This scene is filled with children who are at the peak of athletic prowess. The soccer coach's young son has just scored a hat-trick and holds the cup high as he sits on his teammates' shoulders. A parent whose son had never left the substitute bench approaches the coach and says, "You must be so proud of your boy."

Perhaps the coach had heard some of the comments that parent had made to his son, who sat with shoulders bent, and he replies slowly, "I was proud of him before he could kick a ball, and I will be proud of him if he never touches one again. He's my son."

Acceptance doesn't mean that we do not motivate our children to do better. It doesn't even mean that we don't hope they'll change in some ways. It means that we do not put on them the burden of trying to be somebody they cannot be.

We want them to achieve, but, more than that, we want them to be successful as people. For that, they need a sense of security. And there is no greater security—and nothing more certain to bind a child to his father—than knowing that even if his sister is cleverer, tidier, and more attractive than he, he is loved *anyway*.

Action Page

➪ Share in cooking a meal with your child. You can start younger than you think!

➪ Measure your children's height regularly. Have a chart where you monitor their growth–the back of a cupboard door is a good place.

➪ Try to eat meals together whenever possible.

➪ Watch one of their favorite television programs with them and try to appreciate why *they* like it.

The Sixty-Second Page

When children live with tolerance and fair treatment,
They learn to be patient and fair with others.
When children live with encouragement,
They learn to be confident and secure.
When children live with praise and compliments,
They learn appreciation.
When children live with fairness,
They learn the meaning of justice.
When children live with security,
They learn to have faith.
When children live with approval,
They learn to like themselves.
When children live with unconditional acceptance,
They learn to find love in God and the world.

"Children Learn What They Live"
    (author unknown)[6]

Goal 4
To Praise
My Children

John is your son, and his bedroom is a mess. It has been that way since he moved into it from the maternity ward. At first he threw rattles, toys, and food about the place. Later he moved on to play bricks, broken railway sets, and games with the dice missing.

But he has graduated from all that. He has reached the teenage years. Now there is hardly a rattle, board game, or railway set to be seen, but that may be because it's quite hard to see anything in that clutter.

If you stumbled on this bedroom without warning, your first thought would be to call the police. The room looks as if a manic burglar who has a personal grudge against the occupant has done his worst. The drawers are all open, CDs are scattered over the floor, and there are piles of clothes lying around–like long-forgotten burial mounds. You glance under the bed and immediately regret it. Various life-forms seem to thrive there, several of them in a long-abandoned pile of socks, underwear, and candy wrappers. You think you see something move and get out fast.

Most parents have had to deal with a bedroom like that at some time. How have we tackled it? Normally we have employed the age-old management technique of yelling. We may have yelled for the best part of ten years. It's true there have been small victories, but we may feel that, overall, the strategy doesn't seem to be working.

There are three alternatives:
1. Put a health warning on the door and learn to live with it.
2. Keep yelling.
3. Try another strategy.

The conflict of the bedroom is just one that we regularly fight. There's also the "Battle of Homework Ridge" and "High Noon at Hamster Cage" ("it's *your* hamster, *you* clean it out!"). Regular warfare is wearing, and, more than that, we seem to be constantly nagging.

In fact, so much of the training we give our children is based on catching them doing something wrong and criticizing them for it. But there is another way.

One father shared with me how for years he had been trying to get his ten-year-old son to hold a knife and fork properly. The child normally grabbed the cutlery as if he were an extra on the set of *The Last of the Mohicans*. One day they were together in a restaurant. The child was getting it wrong again, and the father was about to launch into the old tirade when he bit his lip. A little later he noticed that his son was holding his knife and fork correctly. It was probably by accident (he had tried almost every other way) but the father reached over, touched his son's arm, and said, "Great job! You've got it."

He said the next thirty minutes were fascinating as his son tried with every ounce of determination to continue holding those implements correctly. The father had discovered that, although most of us eventually respond to criticism, the faster route is always praise. Not just our homes but our workplaces could be revolutionized by the discovery of that simple principle.

There were at least two elements to that praise. The tongue was part of it. It's easy to fall into the trap of saying to ourselves, *Oh, they know I'm pleased with them.* The power is in *saying* it.

And the hand was involved. In our sophisticated society, we are often embarrassed by touch. If our hand accidentally brushes another hand on a crowded elevator, we immediately apologize as though we have passed on some infectious disease. But touch with our children conveys love, acceptance, and approval.

A boy of fourteen put it like this: "Now that I'm a teenager my parents don't hug me. But when no one was looking I wish they still would."

The heart of this is an attitude that looks for situations in which we can praise our children. In *The One Minute Manager,*[7] Ken Blanchard and Spencer Johnson summarize it like this:

> *Help people reach their full potential*
> *Catch them doing something right.*

The comment came from a woman in her twenties. She was looking back on her teenage years during which she had gotten into a lifestyle that was now exacting a heavy emotional toll on her. She struggled to articulate why she had rebelled so violently. Then she said, "The fastest way to get my dad's attention was to do something wrong."

The power of praise is awesome. There is hardly a person on the face of the earth who does not respond to it. Most of us know how effective it can be in the work situation but forget that, to a child, it can be like rain in the desert.

Praise does so many things at once. It tells us that what we are doing is *right*. It encourages us to do it again. It makes us want to please the person who has encouraged us. And it builds bonds of affection.

It must never be insincere, but it can be given for small victories:

> *"Rachel, thank you for making those visitors feel at home."*
>
> *"John, well done for giving some of your allowance to that Third World project."*
>
> *"Carl, I thought you were going to yell at that referee. I'm proud of you for keeping your cool."*

The principle of catching our children doing something right is a powerful one. But let's try something a little more serious which has in it not just the element of praise but of blame.

> *"Jenny, you've done well to move from a D to a C in math. But I'm disappointed in the rest of your report*

card, not just because of attainment but because of effort. Your progress in school matters to me because I want you to reach your full potential."

We may say "too emotional." I don't think so. But if you disagree you might want to try this instead:

"Jenny, I have to tell you—this is just not good enough! I am ashamed to sign this report card. You are lazy, and if you go on like this you'll be a loser forever! Get out of my sight."

That little episode has in it a father's anger, a racing heartbeat, biting criticism, and a memory that may last a lifetime. Is that emotion enough?

At this stage you have every right to say, "OK, I get the message. I'm going to search for things that I can *genuinely praise my children for.* But what about that bedroom? Tell me something positive I can say."

I have to confess, it's not easy, but how about this . . .

. . . "Son, your ceiling
certainly is tidy!"

Goal 5
To Laugh More with
My Children

When I'm gone and my children talk about me, I would love them to say that I taught them great things: to look at the world with large eyes, to reach their potential, and to care for those who are weak. But I would wonder if I had missed it if they didn't add, "But what we remember, too, is that he was fun to be with."

—A Father

Life is serious. There is pain and sorrow on every hand. There are bills to pay and exams to pass, there is healthy eating to attend to and discipline to be imparted. All that is true; but childhood needs also to be a time of laughter. To see a picture of a child abused or hungry or alone brings tears not just because of the direct pain but because he is being robbed of his childhood and of his right to laugh.

We somehow have to raise children who can cope with the serious issues of life yet can remember years of laughter. That may involve *us* in learning to laugh again.

An anonymous priest looked back on his life and considered how he would do it differently if he could turn back the clock. Here's some of what he said:

*If I had my life over again I would limber up. I
would be sillier than I have been on this trip.*

*I would watch more sunsets. I would do more
walking and looking. I would eat more ice cream
and less beans. I would have more actual troubles
and fewer imaginary ones.*

*You see, I am one of those people who lives life
sensibly, hour after hour, day after day.*

*I've been one of those people who never goes any-
where without a thermometer, a hot water bottle . . .
a raincoat, an aspirin, and a parachute.*

*If I could do it over again, I wouldn't make such
good grades except by accident. I would ride on
more merry-go-rounds.*

I would pick more daisies.

The Power of Fun

When my children were small they used to love having
what we called a "family night." They would drag their
mattresses into our bedroom and sleep on the floor.
But once in a while we would have a "super family
night." That involved us all sleeping on the den floor
together. There are no logical reasons why four people
with perfectly good beds should want to do that, except
that it's fun.

I was once speaking at a conference and I described in a little more detail a "super family night." I
said, "It's wonderful. We all lie there in the dark, with

the fire going, listening to story tapes and eating too much chocolate."

I finished speaking and knew I was in trouble when I saw a woman coming toward me. I have done enough public speaking to be able to recognize that look at one hundred yards. She cornered me and said, "Do you think it's wise to encourage children to eat chocolate just before they go to bed? Their teeth will rot."

That's a kill-joy in action. They smell a little fun and swoop. I wearily explained, "Yes, they did brush their teeth afterward."

But children love those who have the time not only to teach them but to have fun with them.

I would encourage you to surprise your children. I remember on one occasion trying to save a little electricity at home. I threatened my children with all kinds of things, but the lights were still left on—until I put a chart on the wall with every family member's name on it. When you switched off a light that somebody else had forgotten to turn off, you got a mark. After one week the person with the most marks was awarded five points, and we started again. When you hit thirty points, you won a prize.

For months afterward, you only had to leave a light on for five seconds and somebody would leap out from behind the curtains and switch it off. The place was enveloped in darkness. We were all too scared to use electricity!

Now, I know what you're thinking: *It probably only lasted a short while. I'll bet they soon got tired of it.* You're right. But I know this: in ten years time, when somebody talks about saving power, my children will say, "My father was crazy—you'll never guess what he had us doing." And they will laugh at it—again.

Fun rarely has to have a large price tag attached to it. Fun is borrowing a tent and sleeping in the backyard. It's going to the movies on a school night once a year. It's having water fights and saying in traffic, "The next car we pass will be driven by the kind of man that Susan will marry." As the car pulls up next to yours, you all gaze into it. The children laugh wildly, and you try to maintain a little composure.

I suppose there are potential dangers with all of these examples. You could get pneumonia in the backyard, and we know it's not good to stay up late on school nights. During a water fight, water could hit an electric cord and send the whole neighborhood up in flames, and the man in the car could be an ax murderer who jots down your license plate number. But it will probably be OK . . . and you will laugh with your children.

The day will surely come when you will cry with them. They may be thirteen or thirty and you will have your arms around each other as the family goes through some tough time together. There is no home that is immune from such experiences. But home life needs to be a tapestry of tough times and moments of helpless laughter.

When they were very young, you used to tickle them.

Don't ever stop.

Action Page

➪ If your children work hard at something, praise them, even if they fail.

➪ Buy a new board game. Let them win occasionally!

➪ Listen to story tapes with them.

Goal 6
To Set Boundaries

I was at a friend's house when the new kitten was brought home. The three children were incredibly excited, not the least of whom was four-year-old Rebecca. Before the father released the animal from the safety of its basket, he carefully explained the house rules with regard to the new occupant.

"You may pet the cat on its back and tickle its chin. If you are very careful, you can pet its tummy, and as long as you are gentle you may pick her up and cuddle her." It was at this point that the father's voice grew solemn. "But," he said, "under no circumstances must you ever pull her tail. Do you understand all that?" Three small heads nodded in agreement.

The cat was duly lifted out of its carrier and put on the floor. Immediately, Rebecca, with scarcely a hesitation, took three strides toward it and grabbed its tail. She then turned, smiled at her father, and before the dazed parent could move, yanked for all she was worth.

In essence, that child was saying, "You have given me rules and I understand them. But I have decided to test you by breaking them and crossing the boundary. What are you going to do about this?" The child is looking for a reaction. It is vital she is not disappointed.

It is practically a sacred moment, and it will occur in some form with every parent and every child. Life is full of boundaries. If we cross some of them, we'll lose our friends; if we cross others, we may lose our life.

The child, in that instant, was looking to her father to see if the boundaries really mattered. The issue of discipline is a contentious one, and each parent must ultimately decide what form it is to take. But it is vital that it happens. This is not just a matter of training. There is nothing more guaranteed to create insecurity in a child than her believing that there seem to be no boundaries—and even if there are, that nobody really cares if she crosses them.

Military Strategy

All that is true, but it is also true that, if we are called to war occasionally, it is important that we pick the right fights. The constant question needs to be, *Is this a situation that is worth doing battle over?* If not, we risk getting backed into a corner with no way out—and for no good reason. While loving discipline will cement a relationship, unjust or sharp criticism will kill it. There's many a father who has wished he hadn't started World War III over the issue of the color of a pair of jeans when there were so many more important battles to fight.

This is how one father described a battle he wished he'd never entered:

> *My daughter came home one evening with bright orange hair. I hit the roof. My first thought was,* What will people think of us? *I told her she*

would never look like that while she was under my roof and to get it changed. She refused, and I was left with either backing down or making her leave. As it was, we didn't speak for a month. We're fine together now, but I almost lost my daughter over some stupid hair dye.

Very few people enjoy confrontation, but in a father-child relationship there are three elements that can ensure that, if it has to happen, it has the potential to be productive.

Remember how fragile the self-esteem of a child can be. When we discipline we must never attack the *person* of a child—only their behavior. If we hold to that principle we may still have a lot to say about what they've done, but it won't include—"You are *so* stupid!"

Forgiveness. There has to come a point where, no matter how much paint the five-year-old has tipped over onto the new carpet or how deep the hurt the teenager has caused, it can be dealt with and forgotten. None of us can survive if the past is thrown at us every time we make a new mistake.

Vulnerability. Children need to know that their father sometimes gets it wrong. I once heard a father boast, "I have never, nor would I ever, apologize to my son." You can fear a man like that, but it's hard to respect him and even harder to have a deep relationship with him.

The Sixty-Second Page

⏰ "Praise does wonders for the sense of hearing."

⏰ "The fastest way to get my father's attention was to do something wrong."

⏰ "There is nothing more guaranteed to create insecurity in a child than her believing that there seem to be no boundaries."

⏰ "Choose your battles."

⏰ "None of us can survive if the past is thrown at us every time we make a new mistake."

"Bring up a child in the way he should go and when he is old he will not depart from it."
    –The Book of Proverbs

Goal 7
Not to Delegate
the Big Issues

The year is 1895; James is just thirteen. All day he has worked alongside his father—watched the way he held the hammer, copied the style of the blow that forged the iron, and even shod two great horses himself. As he lifts his head and gazes out across the fields, he sees his best friend walking behind his father as they plow together.

For as long as anybody in the village can remember the blacksmith shop and the farm have been there. Generations of fathers have passed the ancient skills on to their children. And as they worked side by side with their sons, they taught them things deeper than ironwork or the way to turn the horse at the edge of the field. They led them week by week and over the years into manhood.

The lessons learned have not always been gained easily. Some in the village remember when Harold, the tanner, died. He was just forty years old, and his son, only a week past fourteen, had taken over the workshop. He was just a child, but now with seven mouths to feed. Of course, for a while the leather wasn't as smooth as when his father had fashioned it, but after a year there wasn't a woman in the town who could tell the difference. And the seven were fed; his father would have been pleased. He had taught him well.

The year is 1995 and James is thirteen. The modern James has not spent time at his father's side today. His father left the house before James awoke, and James has been at school all day. On the way home he stopped for his piano class. As soon as he gets home, he turns on the television and sits glued as it both entertains and educates him.

By the time James goes to bed, he will have experienced a multitude of teachers, both human and electronic. Some will have told him facts about the world that he lives in, and others will have conveyed their feelings. Entwined in the geography will be the question of why people in Ethiopia are hungry; alongside the science will be the big question of where it all came from; and in religious studies, the issue is raised as to what is really important in life. Others will have either tuned or dulled his ear to great music, molded a mind to politics, taught a sexual ethic, and helped create a man.

At nine that evening, he will meet–for the first time that day–his father, who will say, "What did you learn today, Son?" And a thirteen-year-old boy will give the universal answer of the teenager: "Oh, nothing."

But the truth is different. The truth is: "Everything."

Time to Teach

In the film *True Lies,* Arnold Schwarzenegger has a teenage daughter whom he is finding hard to control. One of his colleagues from work explains why he may be finding it so difficult: "You're not her parents any more. Her parents are Axl Rose [the lead singer in the heavy metal rock group "Guns 'n' Roses"] and Madonna. Don't think that the five minutes you spend with her can compete with that kind of bombardment."

If we want our children to accept our values, we have to pass them on. Those values could be spiritual; if I want my children to believe, I need to take time to explain my Christian faith. They may be sexual; if so, I need the courage to talk to them openly about both the wonder and the dangers of sex. If I have things that I believe are right and wrong, I have to let them know what these are. They may reject those values, but if they matter to me, I dare not leave it to others to teach them.

Of course, much of this teaching happens informally, day by day, as they see how we react to situations. In fact, the frightening thing is that, with children, values are more caught than taught. But there will always need to be conversations, debates, and guidance, and all of that takes planning and time.

A letter from a teenager:[8]

Dear Mom and Dad,

There have been times when you say you understand me. But you really don't. There have been times when I tell you about my problems in the hope of your advice or support. But quite often you shrug me off saying, "That's nothing . . . you should have our problems."

It was your responsibility to tell me about sex before I discovered it the wrong way. You may not know it, but I learned sex from the street. Believe me, that's not a good place to learn it.

    John

♦ ♦ ♦

Now James is forty years old, and by his side in the car is a thirteen-year-old child who turns and asks, "Dad, what did your father believe about the world and work and sex and that kind of stuff?" And James will say, "I really don't know—he never told me." And for a brief moment, a faraway look will come into his eye and then vanish as he says, "Come on—you'll be late for your class."

And time will have performed its great trick, and two generations—a hundred and fifty years apart,—will have passed on to their children . . . what their fathers gave to them.

Action Page

➪ Pass on to your children the most significant lesson you learned from your father or an older person you knew as a child.

➪ Teach your children how to handle money; help them prepare a simple income and expenditure budget and keep track of it.

➪ If possible, take your child to the place where you work. Let him sit or stand in your place. Tell him how you spend your day.

Goal 8
To Rediscover
the Ordinary

It was an offer that would bring a gleam to the eye of any child:

> *Visit the zoo! You can wander and explore the exhibits in any way you like. You can even go behind the scenes! Take a trip to Kids' Corner and Storybook Theater. See tiny animals in the nursery and visit the Center for the Protection of Endangered Species.*

> *And that's not all! See our special exhibitions: "Animals in Disguise," "Jaws," and "Creature Features." Your own guide is provided, and you can jump on and off tours and explore things that interest you.*

Then it gave a short note of what you need to get on board this incredible children's experience:

> *A computer: IBM PC or compatible with 80386SX processor or better. Your computer should have:*

> > *2 Mb RAM*
> > *MPC compatible sound card*
> > *MPC compatible CD-ROM drive*
> > *Super VGA Graphics adapter and monitor*
> > *Microsoft compatible mouse recommended*

> *DOS 3.1 or higher*
>
> *Windows 3.1*
>
> *Microsoft Extensions for CD-ROM
> (MSCDEX) 2.2 or higher*

For a child to experience all this wonder, he or she has to be the proud owner of hundreds of dollars worth of equipment. Once they have it, the one ingredient they won't need is *you*.

Of course, you'll need to be involved for a while, but once you've plugged it in and set the thing up, they'll hardly bother you again. In truth, within hours they will be so far ahead that you'll never catch up.

And they will be quiet. When they have finished looking around the zoo, they can slip another disk in and they'll be playing football or going on an Amazon adventure.

Giving Great Gifts

I recently went to a house where a small boy was playing. His computer screen was lifeless—a frame showing some intricate battle between interplanetary forces was frozen until he chose to give it life again. I found him in the tiny garden at the back of the house. He held in his hands a small, square, plastic box. In it he had put some leaves and six caterpillars he had found. As I approached, he lifted the lid gingerly and, as if to prove the size of the haul, counted them out loud.

We sat together and I told him the incredible story of what a caterpillar can become. His eyes were wide with wonder, and, when I suggested that he release them from the relative safety of his box to take their chance in the wild, he didn't seem to mind.

I have found it hard to get that child out of my mind. He seemed to represent a whole generation of children who in material terms have more than any children who have ever lived, yet are so poor. I wondered if he would ever build a tree house, make a dam in a river, or try to knock a can off a wall at ten yards.

And I wondered if he would ever do any of that with his father.

I know that times have changed, and we are foolish if we long for a past "golden era." I also understand why as parents we want to give our children what we can, but Dr. James Dobson has summed up the dilemma: "We are so busy giving our children what we didn't have that we don't have time to give them what we did have."

Your nine-year-old son will forget the television you bought for his bedroom. It is true that it will seem kind to him. It will never say, "Later". It will always say, "Sit down with me now." It will, in the isolation of his room, go about its business of educating him. It was expensive, but it won't be a memory he will cherish.

He will never forget the night that you and he slept in the backyard in an old tent that somebody lent you. He will remember the sense of thrill as you both ate too many marshmallows and how he felt when the battery in the flashlight failed and it was darker than he had ever known. And when he is old he will still remember it.

And there it is—the great dilemma of being a parent in a society where love can too easily be measured in presents, while the real craving of children of any generation is a father's *presence*.

I recently watched a father and his son playing catch on a beach. It was in many ways a typical game: every time one of them missed, the ball rolled to the very end of the beach and needed a marathon runner to get it back; poor fielding meant that it often went into the sea and one of them would risk life and limb to retrieve it. No marketing whiz-kid will ever show an interest in packaging this pastime, and it will never be advertised on television, complete with background music and special effects. Yet this father and son played for hours, and the laughter could be heard a mile away.

And that's how it should be—whether it's bedtime stories with a toddler, treasure hunts with a nine-year-old, or drinking coffee and listening to music with a teenager—the poorest father can give the best gifts.

Action Page

⇨ Catch your children doing something right–
  today!

⇨ Try to avoid having a television in your child's
  bedroom.

⇨ Make a list of values that are important to you.
  Ask yourself whether you are effectively passing
  those on to your child.

⇨ Discover Legos–they seem to work with children
  from 0 to 100!

Goal 9
To Forge a Strong Relationship with My Children

We are almost at our last goal, but we are very near where we began. The heart of *The Sixty Minute Father* is a commitment to build bonds with our children that will last. That is something most fathers want; the only problem is that no relationship in the world has been built without giving it time.

I sometimes hear fathers say, "I can't give my children quantity time, so I give them quality time." I understand that, but the problem with communicating with children is that often you have to put in a lot of quantity so that the quality can really happen.

A father may have spent two hours helping a teenage daughter hang some pictures in her room. He's not brilliant at this, evidenced by the fact that the wall seems to have several new indentations which are nowhere near the pictures. Nevertheless, they are hanging there—for now. It would be hard to describe that experience as "quality time," but as the father puts away his hammer and tightens the sticking plaster on his thumb, his daughter says, "Dad, can I talk to you about something?"

For some time I have been involved in organizing vacations for parents, including single parents and their children, but with a difference. The whole point of these weeks has been to develop stronger bonds between parents and their children. One week is called "Dads and Lads." Fathers come from all walks of life. I have seen fathers and sons climb together, fish together, and *talk* together. I remember a father who lived separately from his ten-year-old son taking me aside and, with a face filled with excitement, saying, "My son hugged me tonight."

The week had given this father and his son both quantity and quality of something they needed almost as much as breath: time together.

One of the greatest joys for me has been to "date" my daughter, Katie. Since she was twelve, we have spent evenings together; it could be a cup of coffee, a pizza, sometimes a film, or even just a walk.

Those evenings have been a lifesaver for us. They are away from the interruptions of the home and provide an "adult" setting so that Katie has felt they were special. We've often sat with one Coke for an hour or more—so they needn't be expensive—but those times helped us build our relationship.

My son, Lloyd, and I have just started a similar event. We've found places to drink coffee, talk—and play pool!

All this is especially hard for fathers who *have* to be away from home a great deal; if they want a job, it means that they are on the road. One father in this situation told me how he coped. He said, "When you have to be away from home, you have to work harder at relationships. I let my children know in a dozen ways I'd rather be with them. And when I am home, I let *nothing* rob me of that time with them. They get my undivided attention. When I get home I don't want them thinking about whether I have bought them large presents; I want them to be excited about seeing *me.*"

Our children crave our time. As I was writing this book, a man came into my study. He is forty years of age. As he flipped through some of the draft pages he said, "When I was in school I always wanted my father to watch me play rugby. I was never able to tell him how badly I wanted that. He came . . . once."

Consider this definition of a grandmother by a nine-year-old girl:

> *Grandmothers don't have to do anything except to be there. If they take us for walks, they slow down past things like pretty leaves and caterpillars, and they never say "hurry up."*
>
> *Usually grandmothers are fat but not too fat to tie your shoes.*
>
> *They wear glasses and funny underwear and they can take their teeth and gums out.*
>
> *Grandmothers don't have to be clever,*
>
> *Just be able to answer questions like "Why isn't God married?" and "Why do dogs chase cats?"*
>
> *Grandmothers don't talk baby talk to us like visitors do because they know it's hard for us to understand it.*

When they read to us, they don't skip pages, or mind if it's the same story over and over again.

Everybody should have a grandmother, especially if you don't have television

. . . because they're the only grown-ups that have time.[9]

Action Page

⇨ Plan as soon as possible a half day with your child when you can spend time alone doing ordinary things together.

⇨ Never give up on the relationship with your child, whatever age they are—even if they have left home under a cloud.

⇨ Take heart from the man who said, "When I got married I had four theories of child-rearing and no children. Now I have four children and no theories!"

The Sixty-Second Page

⏰ "If we want our children to accept our values, we have to pass them on."

⏰ "We are so busy giving our children what we didn't have that we don't have time to give them what we did have."

⏰ "Grandmothers . . . slow down past things like pretty caterpillars, and they never say 'hurry up.'"

⏰ "The problem with communicating with children is that you have to put in a lot of quantity so that the quality can really happen."

⏰ "And that's how it should be—the poorest father can give the best gifts."

Goal 10
The Final Goal

We have arrived at the tenth and final goal. It is in many senses the culmination of all the others. Before we discover it, let's pause for a while.

I want to say something to the father whose children have already left home. That can be such a difficult time. One parent put it like this: "Suddenly they were gone, and I walked past a *too-tidy bedroom.*"

It would be easy for any of us in this situation to be filled with regret, to say, "If I could only turn back the clock and begin again." We each need to remember that the father-child bond is very deep; it is almost never too late to begin building a relationship or to try rebuilding one that is lost. It may mean swallowing a little pride, but that's a small price.

I once met a father who did just that. His daughter had rebelled, turned her back on everything her father believed and wanted for her. There had been many quarrels, but one night a door slammed and . . . silence. She left home; they didn't speak for six months. But the day came when he felt he must talk to her. He called her; this is what he said:

> *Cathy, you have turned your back on everything I have ever believed and wanted for you. I found that so hard. I had so many dreams for your future. But I have been wrong. Those desires for you have not*

diminished one bit, but I have realized that it is your life. Please forgive me if I have tried to run it for you.

I want you to know that this home is always open to you. It is your home. Forgive me if I have ever made you feel otherwise.

I love you and nothing you ever do or don't do will change that. I am for you.

You may be reading this at the very beginning of your role as father. Let me summarize the heart of this little book for you as you begin the incredible task of parenthood.

If you are fortunate enough to have a job, do it with all your heart. But remember that although it is a vital part of your life, it is only a part, and although you may rise to great heights, somebody else will one day take your place at the work bench or at the head of the boardroom table. Nobody *will* ever *take your place as the father of the child you are now cradling in your arms. You may well work for the best part of half a century, but the time you have been given to pass on the things that matter to your child is so very limited. There will be many demands on your time, and you will not always be able to give your children the time they ask. But so far as is possible, count the days.*

Try not to miss one of them.

This has been a book about the relationship between a father and his child, but, of course, the heart of the matter is deeper than that. On St. Valentine's day, Dr. Benjamin Salk, a family psychologist, was being interviewed on a morning TV program. The interviewer asked him two very profound questions:

1. "Is everybody born with the capacity to love?" Dr. Salk answered, "Yes."

2. Then he was asked, "Then why don't we have more love in the world?" This is what he answered: "Even though we are born with the capacity to love, we need to learn how to love." Then he turned to the camera, looked millions of viewers in the eye, and said, "The greatest thing you parents can do for your children is to love each other."[10]

Such love does not always come easily. It is my belief that every marriage goes through a time when at least one of the partners does not feel in love and everything screams out, *Let go—it's over.* I see too much pain on a daily basis to believe these are easy issues, but I know that sometimes love is an act of the will and that it can still be a good reason to try again, "for the sake of the children."

I don't see many letters from children, but there's one that I can't get out of my mind. It's from an eight-year-old boy.

> *My dad doesn't love my mom any more and he's found somebody else. But he doesn't know how sad it's made us, 'cos if he did he would have never gone.*

So what is the final goal? In many ways it is the

hardest of all. Everything that has gone before is simply a preparation for it.

To find it we go to a poem. A father is teaching his daughter to ride a bicycle. He holds the back of the saddle to steady her as she wobbles her way down the road. She finds the task difficult, but so long as the father's hand is there, she can ride.

The key is in that father's hand. It gives her the security she needs to go a little faster, to sit a little more upright. She may never know that occasionally he took his hand away, and then quickly put it back before she could know. But the father knows that the hand is on the saddle for just a moment and that the day soon will come when she won't need him in quite the same way . . .

> *Tomorrow though I will run behind,*
> *Arms out to catch her, she'll tilt then balance wide*
> *Of my reach, till distance makes her small,*
> *. . . I stop and know*
> *That to teach her I had to follow*
> *And when she learned . . .*
> *I had to let her go.*[11]

. . . And that's the final goal.

The task of fatherhood is not an easy one. Somebody has put it well: "There is no pain like parental pain." The truth is, with all our failures and inability to be the kind of fathers we want to be, these children matter to us, more than almost anything else in the world. And there are pitfalls galore. On the one hand is the danger of not giving our children the time and attention they need, and on the other, the peril of being so consumed with them that we drive ourselves crazy and suffocate them emotionally.

But we also have the incredible privilege of the sheer joy and—dare I say it—fun they can bring into our lives and, even more, of being part of molding a life. And the life we mold will almost certainly one day step into those same parental shoes. And there is the great challenge: not just to be an effective father for the sake of our children, but for the sake of *their* children.

For a task so great we each need all the help we can get. One night, when my son was very small, I was saying prayers with him. The next day I was due to fly abroad to address an international law conference. It was a prestigious event, and I was more than a little nervous. I have prayed many prayers for him, but on this occasion I asked him to utter one for me. This is what he said:

> *Dear Lord, please help my dad to be brave, and not to make too many mistakes.*

It's not a bad prayer for every father.

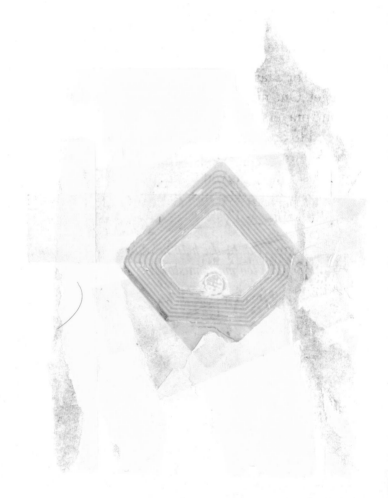

Notes

1. Robert Herrick, "To the Virgins, to Make Much of Time," A. Quiller-Couch (ed.), *The Oxford Book of English Verse, 1250-1918* (Oxford: Oxford University Press, 1939), 274.

2. Robert Fulghum, "The Lessons of the Sandpile," *All I Really Need to Know I Learned in Kindergarten* (London: Collins, 1990), 6.

3. Harry Chapin, "Cat's in the Cradle." Copyright 1974 by Story Songs Ltd.

4. U. Bronfenbrenner, "The Origins of Alienation," *Scientific American,* August 1974.

5. *Young Peoples Relationships, Lifestyle and Sexual Attitudes,* MARC Europe Report by Boyd Myers, Agape, 1991.

6. Dorothy Law Nolte, "Children Learn What They Live." This poem is often published under "author unknown" and appears to be in the public domain.

7. Kenneth Blanchard and Spencer Johnson, *The One Minute Manager* (London: Harper Collins Publishers, 1994).

8. Josh McDowell and Dick Day, *Why Wait? What You Need to Know about the Teen Sexuality Crises* (San Bernardino, Calif.: Here's Life Publishers, 1990), 379.

9. "What's a Grandmother?" submitted by nurse Juanita Nelson to the employee newspaper at Childrens Hospital, Los Angeles.

10. Josh McDowell and Dick Day, *How to Be a Hero to Your Kids* (Dallas: Word Publishing, 1991), 126.

11. Poem adapted from Wyatt Prunty, "Learning the Bicycle (for Heather)," *The American Scholar,* 58, No. 1, (Winter 1989), 122.